Passing Journey

A.L. Burgess Jr.

This book is a work of fiction. References to real people, events, establishments, organizations, or locales are intended only to provide a sense of authenticity, and are used to advance the fictional narrative. All other characters, and all incidents and dialogue, are drawn from the author's imagination and are not to be construed as real.

Passing Journey
Copyright © 2020 by A. L. Burgess Jr.

The right of A. L. Burgess Jr. to be identified as the author of this work has been asserted by him in accordance with the Copyright, Designs and Patents Act, 1988.

All rights reserved. No part of this book may be used or reproduced in any manner whatsoever without written permission of the publisher. For information or extended permissions, please contact the publisher at:

www.ALBurgessJr.com.

ISBN: 978-0-9915621-8-3 (trade p,bk)
ISBN: 978-0-9915621-9-0 (ebook)

Illustrations by:
Kashif Qasim

First Edition, 2020

For those who have lost—

Passing Journey

"Wake up!" the animals whopped.

"Time to get up, Chris!"

"It's been so long!" Chris exclaimed, excited to see the family's beloved pets. "What are you doing here?"

"We knew you needed help," woofed Rex the dog. "So we came right away!"

"Help?" Chris muttered and looked at the dark forest in front of the group. "What am I doing here?"

Sandy the rabbit sniffed the air.

"You're starting your journey."

"We're all coming with you," meowed Bella the cat.

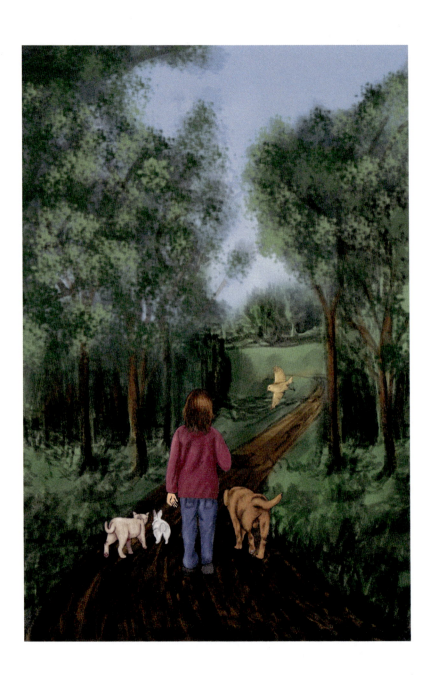

"What kind of journey is this?" asked Chris.

"One we must all take," chirped Simon the bird.

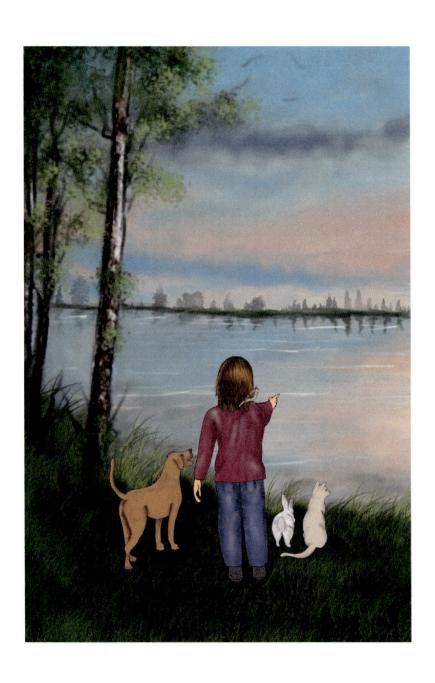

"I remember this place!" Chris excitedly called out. "Rex, do you remember?" Chris asked, pointing to a spot near the water. "We played fetch over there."

Rex woofed out, "That was a great day!"

"This party was fun!" said Chris.

"You got in trouble for eating the cake, Bella."

"It's okay," Bella meowed.

"We all get in trouble sometimes. Besides," Bella purred while licking her paw, "it was good cake."

"This is where I got you, Simon," Chris said.

"I'm sorry you had to live in that cage."

"It's okay," chirped Simon.

"Besides, I was happy to be with you."

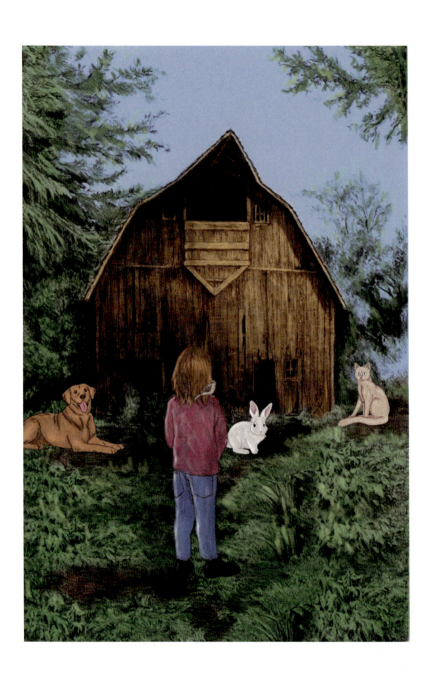

"I'm so sorry, Sandy," lamented Chris, gazing sadly at the bunny. "I took you away from your family."

"You gave me a good home," Sandy sniffed her reply. "I'm glad it was you."

"I don't feel good about this place," Chris said.

"Yes," the pets said in unison.

"You fell out of that tree and got hurt really bad."

"I remember," Chris said, recalling the pain.

"What happened to the leaves?"

"Trees don't live forever," Rex woofed.

"I've never been here before," Chris said.

"This is a new place for you," chirped Simon.

"This is a new place for all of us," meowed Bella.

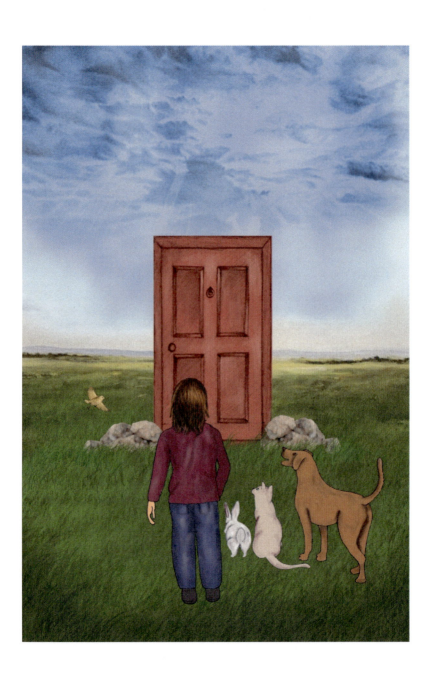

"What is it?" asked Chris.

"Open it and find out," they responded.

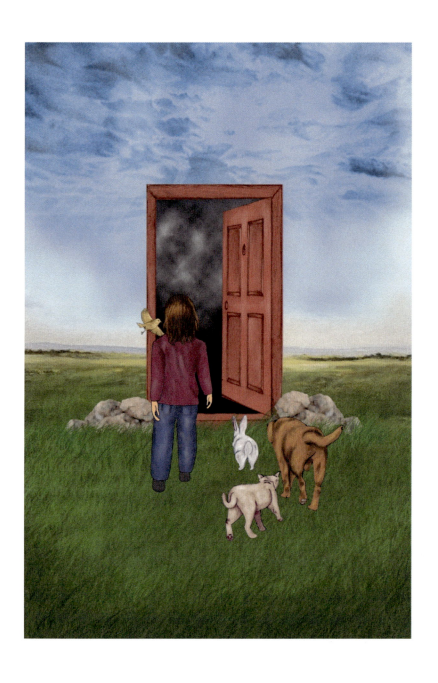

Chris took a deep breath. "I'm really scared."

"We know," Rex woofed in a reassuring tone.

"Be brave, Chris. We're here for you."

"I hear voices," Chris said.

"They sound friendly."

"Old family and friends," Bella meowed.

"I'll go first," sniffed Sandy.

She hopped up to the opaque threshold and cocked an ear. Satisfied that it was safe, Sandy jumped through the doorway and stared back at the group.

"See, I did it!" she said, and disappeared from view.

"I will go next," Simon chirped boldly.

He flapped his wings for a moment, hovering in midair, and then darted through the threshold.

"I made it!" he said, and disappeared from view.

"I guess it's my turn," Bella meowed.

She rubbed up against Chris and sauntered her way across the hazy threshold. Bella stood for a moment, looking back at Chris and Rex.

"See?" she meowed. "Piece of cake."

She flicked her tail and disappeared.

"I don't want to go, Rex," a teary-eyed Chris said, staring down at the dog who had been the most faithful companion Chris had ever known.

"I know," woofed Rex. "Why don't we go together?"

Chris nodded and placed a hand on Rex's back. The old dog made his way slowly to the doorway. Chris followed alongside patting Rex gently as they walked. Together, the friends crossed the threshold and disappeared from sight.

Made in the USA
Monee, IL
13 January 2022